Lyrical Landscapes

11 EXPRESSIVE PIANO PIECES IN A VARIETY OF STYLES
MIKE SPRINGER

Foreword

Lyrical Landscapes, Book 2 is a collection of expressive pieces in a variety of styles and tempos. It was written to provide opportunities for early intermediate to intermediate students to develop skills in projecting lyrical, melodic lines. While many of the pieces were inspired by music from the Romantic era, lyric qualities are also applied to a variety of more contemporary styles.

From slow ballads to upbeat tempos, these pieces allow pianists the opportunity to develop a deeper musical awareness through the use of technical control, rubato, and subtle tempo changes. These pieces were composed so students not only enjoy performing the music, but grow musically along the way.

Mike Springer

In memory of Madeline Marie Wermuth

Contents

Alfred Music
P.O. Box 10003
Van Nuys, CA 91410-0003
alfred.com

ISBN-10: 1-4706-3897-5
ISBN-13: 978-1-4706-3897-9

Cover Photos:
Water Lily Pond: © Getty Images / irakite • Gray and White Castle: © Pexels.com • Balloons: © Getty Images / VladyslavDanilin

Campfire by the Lake

Mike Springer

Fond Farewell

Mike Springer

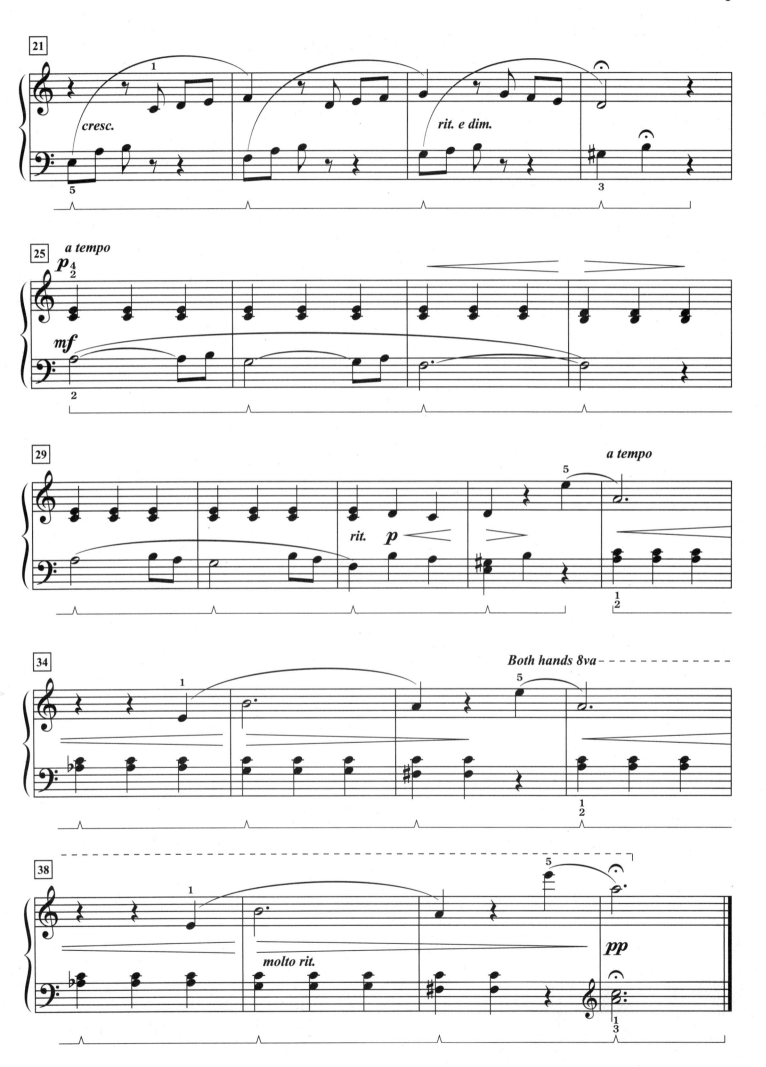

French Café

Mike Springer

Jardin de Provence
(Garden of Provence)

Mike Springer

9

Medieval Castle

Mike Springer

Mockingbirds

Mike Springer

Mountain Breeze

Mike Springer

Royal Procession

Mike Springer

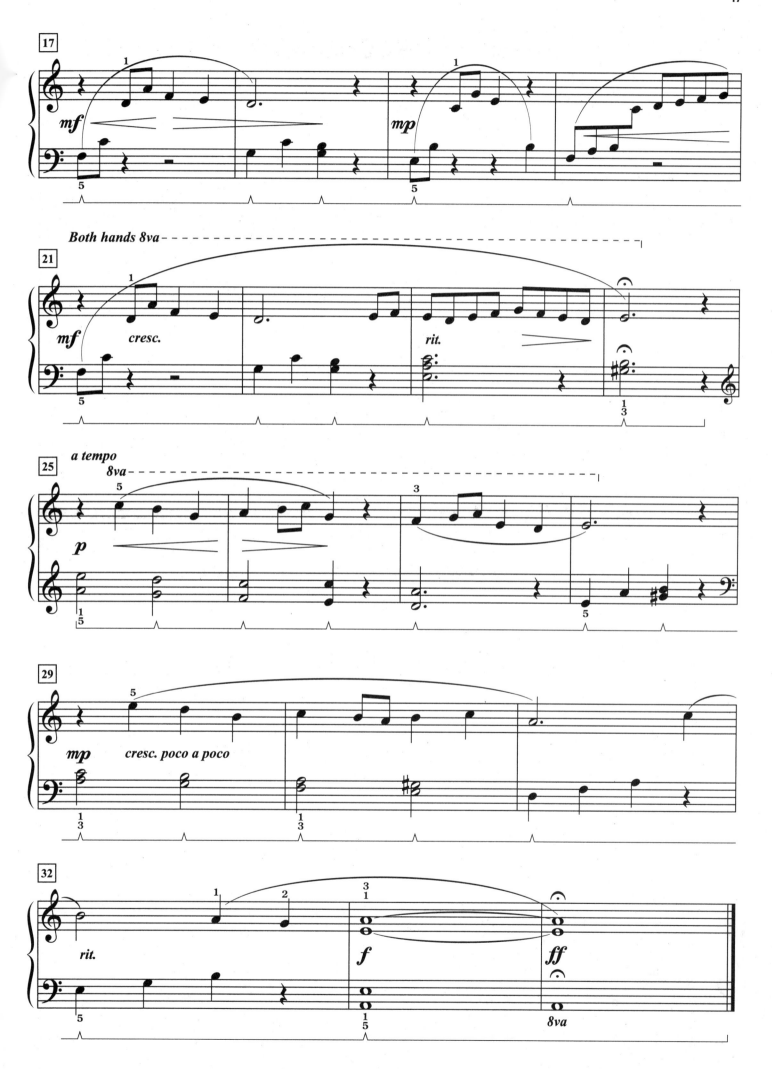

Spring Blossoms

Mike Springer

Starlight Reverie

Mike Springer

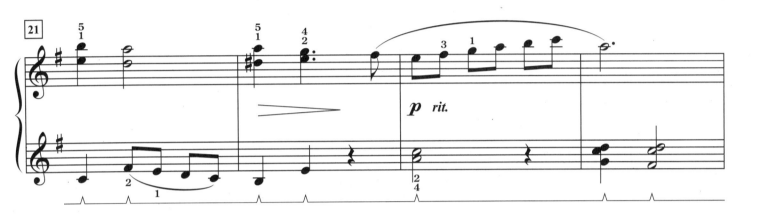

A little slower

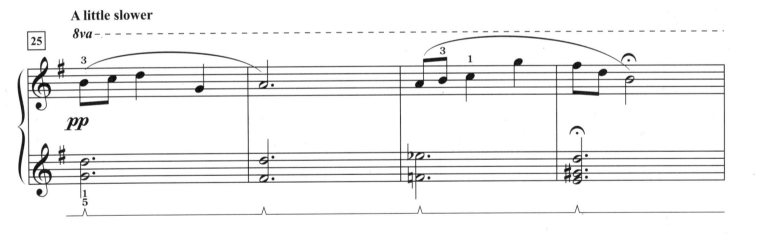

Much slower, with freedom

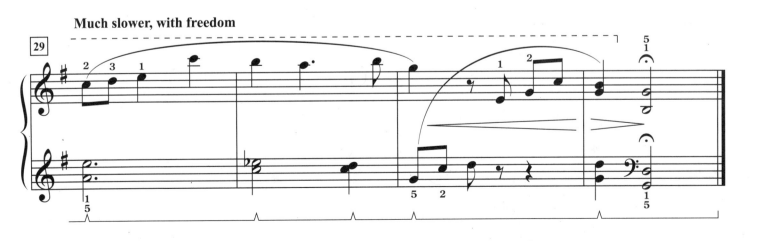

Morning Meditation

Mike Springer

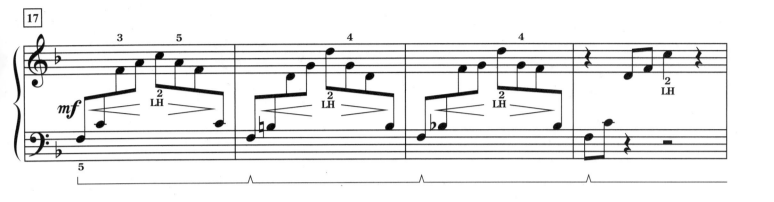

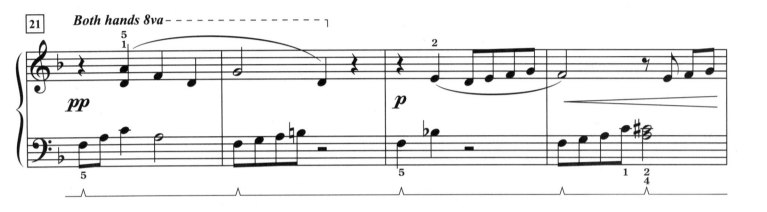

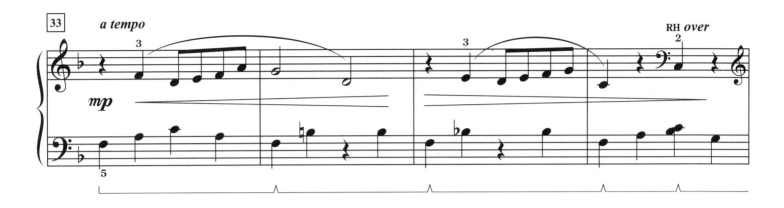

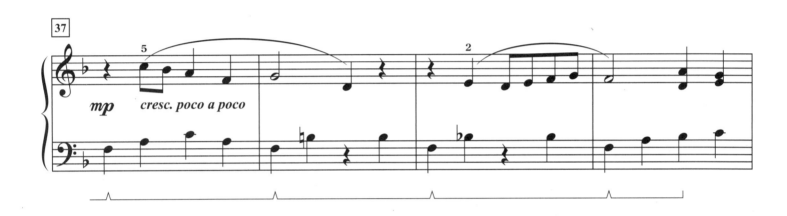

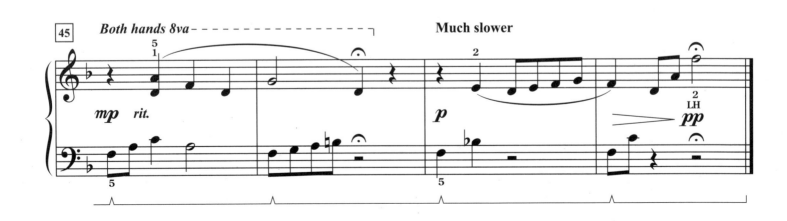